Ingredients for a Healthy Life

FANTASTIC FRUIT Recipes

Gareth Stevens
PUBLISHING

By Kristen Rajczak

Please visit our website, www.garethstevens.com. For a free color catalog of all our high-quality books, call toll free 1-800-542-2595 or fax 1-877-542-2596.

Library of Congress Cataloging-in-Publication Data

Rajczak, Kristen.
Fantastic fruit recipes / by Kristen Rajczak.
   p. cm. — (Ingredients for a healthy life)
Includes index.
ISBN 978-1-4824-0566-8 (pbk.)
ISBN 978-1-4824-0568-2 (6-pack)
ISBN 978-1-4824-0565-1 (library binding)
1. Fruit — Juvenile literature. 2. Cooking (Fruit) — Juvenile literature. I. Rajczak, Kristen. II. Title.
TX397.R35 2014
641.3—dc23

First Edition

Published in 2015 by
Gareth Stevens Publishing
111 East 14th Street, Suite 349
New York, NY 10003

Copyright © 2015 Gareth Stevens Publishing

Designer: Andrea Davison-Bartolotta
Editor: Kristen Rajczak

Photo credits: Cover, back cover, pp. 1, 3, 9, 11, 13, 15, 17, 19, 21–24 (strawberry background) vic dd/Shutterstock.com; cover, p. 1 (salad) vanillaechoes/Shutterstock.com; cover, pp. 1 (smoothie, pie), 8, 9 (juice, yogurt), 14, 15, 17, 21 (arrows) iStockphoto/Thinkstock; p. 4 (fruit) Hayati Kayhan/Shutterstock.com; p. 4 (notebook) mexrix/Shutterstock.com; p. 5 Fuse/Getty Images; p. 6 (tomato) djgis/Shutterstock.com; p. 6 (squash) Peter Zijlstra/Shutterstock.com; p. 6 (cucumber) orion/Shutterstock.com; p. 7 Nikolay Petkov/Shutterstock.com; p. 9 (smoothie) Vitalfoto/Shutterstock.com; p. 9 (bananas) digitalvox/Shutterstock.com; p. 10 Brand X Pictures/Thinkstock; p. 11 (all) panda3800/Shutterstock.com; p. 12 valigloo/Shutterstock.com; p. 13 Zoonar/Thinkstock; pp. 16–17 D7INAMI7S/Shutterstock.com; p. 18 (kumquat, lychee) Anna Kucherova/Shutterstock.com; p. 18 (star fruit) Viktar Malyshchyts/Shutterstock.com; p. 19 Christopher Halloran/Shutterstock.com; p. 20 Nancy Kennedy/Shutterstock.com; p. 21 (girl) Photodisc/Thinkstock.

Printed in the United States of America

CPSIA compliance information: Batch #CS15GS: For further information contact Gareth Stevens, New York, New York at 1-800-542-2595.

Contents

Recipes in this book may use knives, mixers, and hot stove tops. Ask for an adult's help when using these tools.

Words in the glossary appear in **bold** type the first time they are used in the text.

Fun with Fruit

What's your favorite fruit? From juicy watermelon and tart cranberries to crisp apples and sweet peaches, fruit comes in many shapes, sizes, and flavors. Many people enjoy eating fruit on its own. That's good to do since fruit has many health benefits.

However, there are tons of **recipes** you can make to include fruit in your **diet**, too. Keep reading to learn some awesome ways to eat fruit every day—and the reasons why you should!

Do You Have Allergies?

The recipes in this book may use **ingredients** that contain or have come into contact with nuts, gluten, dairy products, and other common causes of **allergies**. If you have any food allergies, please ask a parent or teacher for help when cooking and tasting!

Did you know that many fruit-flavored products, such as grape popsicles or cherry fruit snacks, have no fruit in them?

5

What's a Fruit?

Fruit's main job isn't to make us healthier. It's to hold the seeds of the plants it grew from. Some fruits, like cherries, are called stone fruits. These have one big seed, or pit, at their center. Oranges, on the other hand, have seeds throughout their flesh.

Since a fruit is a plant body that grows to **protect** and spread a plant's seeds, it's strange to think that farmers have found ways to grow fruits without seeds. Today, seedless oranges and watermelon are common.

CHEW ON THIS!

When is a vegetable not a vegetable? When it's a fruit! Though we call them veggies, cucumbers, tomatoes, and squash are all fruits by the scientific definition.

squash, cucumber, and tomatoes

There are so many kinds of fruit to try!

7

Fresh vs. Frozen

It happens to everyone. You buy a pint of strawberries and a week later, they're covered in white fuzz. What happened?

As soon as fruit is picked, it starts breaking down. Most fruits travel to stores on refrigerated trucks so they can stay fresh for as long as possible. Others are quickly frozen. Don't worry—the fruits are frozen when they're at their ripest and offer many of the same health benefits that fresh fruit does.

CHEW ON THIS!

Raisins are a fruit! They're grapes that have been dried. Dried cherries, plums, and apricots are also very tasty. Try to keep your serving size to only about ¼ cup because these have a lot of sugar in them.

frozen berries

Super Fruit Smoothie

makes 2 big servings or 4 smaller servings

Ingredients:

1 cup frozen cherries
1 cup frozen pineapple
1/2 frozen banana (peel before freezing)
1 cup orange juice
1/2 cup low-fat yogurt

Directions:

1. Mix the orange juice and yogurt in a blender.
2. Add the frozen fruit. Blend until smooth. If your blender has trouble mixing them all or the smoothie looks too thick, add another 1/2 cup of orange juice or water.
3. Serve immediately or store covered in the fridge. The smoothie will keep for about a day and just need a quick stir.

Fruit smoothies make a great breakfast, especially on a hot day. Ask an adult to help you use the blender—then share your creation!

orange juice

yogurt

# Superfruits!

All fruits are good for you, but they don't all offer the same **nutrients**. Because of the different **vitamins** and **minerals** in fruits, it's smart—and tasty—to eat fruits of many colors! In general, the darker the color of the fruit, the more nutrients it has to offer.

Fruits are a good source of carbohydrates. Your body uses these nutrients to make energy. A piece of fruit would be a great snack to eat before a soccer game or dance class!

CHEW ON THIS!

Fiber is the part of plants people can't **digest**. Sometimes called "roughage," fiber helps move food through the body and pass it out as waste. Fruits are a good source of fiber!

Eating fruit may help stop you from getting certain diseases, such as cancer and heart disease. It also aids in keeping a healthy weight.

NUTRIENT	FUNCTION	WHAT TO EAT
folic acid	helps the body make red blood **cells** and skin cells; aids in strengthening bones; keeps nerves working well	strawberries, bananas, melons, lemons, pineapples
magnesium	maintains muscle and nerve activities; aids in strengthening bones; helps keep blood sugar levels and blood pressure normal	bananas, raisins, raspberries, watermelons
potassium	maintains normal blood pressure; keeps kidneys working correctly	papayas, cantaloupes, dried plums, oranges, kiwifruits
vitamin A	maintains eye health; aids in cell growth; helps the heart, lungs, and kidneys work correctly	apricots, cantaloupes, grapefruits, watermelons
vitamin C	protects the body and cells from disease and damage	strawberries, oranges, kiwifruits, cranberries, limes

Have an Apple

People have been eating apples for more than 2,000 years! As Europeans settled the Americas, they brought this juicy fruit with them. Today, apples are grown across North America, but the Pacific Northwest is known for growing especially beautiful fruits.

The old saying "an apple a day keeps the doctor away" may be true! Apples are a good source of fiber and vitamins A and C, as well as substances called antioxidants (an-tee-AHK-suh-duhnts). Antioxidants help protect cells from damage, and they're present in many fruits.

CHEW ON THIS!

There are thousands of kinds of apples. They fall into three general groups: cider apples, cooking apples, and dessert apples.

Classic Apple Pie

Makes about 8 servings

Ingredients:

10 cups peeled and thinly sliced Granny Smith apples (about 3 pounds)

3/4 cup sugar

1 1/2 tablespoons flour

1 teaspoon ground cinnamon

1/2 teaspoon salt

1/4 teaspoon ground nutmeg

1 tablespoon chilled butter, cut into small pieces

2 9-inch prepared piecrusts

Making your own piecrust can be pretty hard. This recipe calls for a crust you can buy in your grocery store's refrigerated section. If you'd like to make your own, there are lots of piecrust recipes online—or your grandma might have one!

Directions:

1. Preheat oven to 425 degrees.
2. Mix apples with sugar, flour, cinnamon, salt, and nutmeg.
3. Lightly spray a 9-inch pie pan with cooking spray. Lay one of the prepared piecrusts in the pan, gently fitting it to the sides and bottom.
4. Spoon the apple filling into the piecrust. Sprinkle the small pieces of butter over the top.
5. Place the second piecrust over the filling. Use your fingers to pinch the edges of the top crust and bottom crust together.
6. Cut a few slits in the top crust to let steam escape.
7. Place the pie on a baking sheet and bake for 10 minutes. Lower the oven temperature to 350 degrees and bake for another 40 minutes, until the top is lightly browned.
8. Allow the pie to cool before cutting.

Strawberry Fields

Nothing says summer like the first pint of homegrown strawberries from the local market. Native to the Americas, strawberries are now grown all over the world.

Aside from giving us lots of beneficial vitamins and minerals, strawberries are very useful in the kitchen. They can be eaten fresh, perhaps sliced on cereal or yogurt. They can be baked into pies and breads. Strawberries are fairly easy to turn into a delicious jam and can even be made into sweet, cold soup!

strawberry field

CHEW ON THIS!

Berries, such as raspberries and blueberries, are especially high in antioxidants. Scientists believe these compounds help the body fight disease and repair itself.

Strawberry and Spinach Salad

makes 2 servings

Ingredients:

Dressing:
4 tablespoons balsamic vinegar
2 tablespoons extra-virgin olive oil
a pinch of salt and pepper

Salad:
1 cup sliced strawberries
1/4 cup very thinly sliced red onion
3 cups baby spinach, washed and dried
1/4 cup chopped walnuts, almonds, or pecans
1/4 cup crumbled feta cheese

Strawberries are delicious and good for you on their own, but add spinach to the mix and you have a healthy salad! Would you like to have this for dinner? Add some grilled chicken on top.

Directions:

1. To make the dressing, measure the balsamic vinegar and extra-virgin olive oil into a jar with a lid. Add the salt and pepper. Put the lid on the jar and shake it up.

2. Place your spinach in a big mixing bowl. Pour the dressing over the top and toss to coat the leaves.

3. Divide the spinach between two plates. Add half of the strawberries, onion, nuts, and cheese to each. If you don't like onion, you can leave it out!

Citrus Fruits

Citrus fruits, such as lemons, limes, grapefruit, and oranges, are among some of the most popular flavors used in the United States. Think of the cool, refreshing tastes of key lime pie, orange sherbet, and lemon ice! There are so many ways to use the juices of citrus fruits, such as mixing them with olive oil in salad dressings or for seasoning fish or vegetables.

Lucky for citrus fruit lovers, these fruits are full of folic acid, potassium, and of course, vitamin C!

CHEW ON THIS!

Fruit juices can count toward your servings of fruit every day. Be sure you are drinking 100 percent fruit juice, which can give you important vitamins and minerals. Don't forget to eat whole fruit for its fiber, too.

Lemonade

makes 6 servings

Ingredients:

1 cup freshly squeezed lemon juice (from about 6 lemons)
4 cups cold water, plus 1 cup
1/2 cup honey

Directions:

1. Pour 1 cup water into a small pan on the stovetop. Add honey. Stir while it heats and comes to a boil.
2. Pour the water and honey mixture into a pitcher.
3. Stir in the 4 cups of cold water and lemon juice.
4. Chill in the fridge for about 2 hours.

You can buy lemonade at the store, but it's much healthier when you make it yourself! This refreshing drink takes a bit of work, so ask for an adult's help when juicing the lemons and using the stove.

Fruits Around the World

Apples and bananas are two of the most common fruits eaten in the United States. But so many more are found and enjoyed around the world! Here are just a few:

- **star fruit:** Found in Indonesia, India, and Sri Lanka, this funny-looking fruit tastes a bit like apple, pineapple, and kiwi combined.

- **lychee:** This fruit is found in China and India. The inside feels somewhat like a grape.

- **kumquat:** Also native to China, this fruit grows on a tree related to that of citrus fruits.

CHEW ON THIS!

Did you know the avocado is a fruit, too? Avocados are grown in Florida and California, but Mexico provides more than half of the avocados sold in the United States.

Fantastic Fruit Pizza

Makes 6 big servings

Ingredients:

Crust:
1 cup all-purpose flour
1 cup whole-wheat flour
1/2 cup sugar
1 teaspoon baking powder
1/2 cup (1 stick) of butter, plus 2 tablespoons
2 eggs
1 teaspoon vanilla extract

Have you ever had pizza for dessert? This cool recipe makes a good—and good-for-you—treat. You can use any combination of fruit you have at home.

Topping:
1 1/2 cups vanilla Greek yogurt
fruit (sliced strawberries, blueberries, kiwifruit, pineapple, or your favorite)

Directions:

1. Use a food processor to mix the flours, sugar, baking powder, and butter until it looks crumb-like.
2. In a separate bowl, whisk together the eggs and vanilla. Pour this into the food processor and mix until a lump of slightly crumbly dough forms.
3. Grease a cookie sheet or pizza pan. Press the dough onto your pan evenly.
4. Bake for 6 to 8 minutes. Don't let the crust brown or your pizza will crumble easily.
5. Let the crust cool.
6. Spread the yogurt onto the cooled crust. Then, arrange the fruit on top. Or, cut into as many pieces as you would like. Then, let people add their favorite fruit toppings to a slice!

19

A What?

Have you ever heard of a pluot? Or a grapple? The first is a plum-apricot, and the second is a grape-apple. Scientists have found ways to cross fruit plants to make new fruits. Some people like these **hybrids**. Others think their names, like tangelo (a tangerine crossed with a pomelo or grapefruit), just sound silly.

Whatever side you're on, fruits are some of the healthiest snacks around. Grabbing a pluot to eat with your breakfast is a great idea—even if it has a funny name!

pluots

Healthy Reasons to Eat Fruit

Vitamins and minerals aid in everyday body functions.

Fiber moves food through the digestive system..

Antioxidants aid in cell protection and repair.

Carbohydrates deliver lots of energy to the body.

Glossary

allergy: a body's sensitivity to usually harmless things in the surroundings, such as dust, pollen, or mold

cell: the smallest basic part of a living thing

diet: the food one usually eats

digest: to break down food inside the body so that the body can use it

hybrid: the offspring of two animals or plants of different kinds

ingredient: a food that is mixed with other foods

mineral: a substance important in small quantities for the nutrition of animals

nutrient: something a living thing needs to grow and stay alive

protect: to keep safe

recipe: an explanation of how to make food

vitamin: a substance important in small quantities for the nutrition of animals

For More Information

BOOKS

Cleary, Brian P. *Apples, Cherries, Red Raspberries: What Is in the Fruit Group?* Minneapolis, MN: Millbrook Press, 2011.

Kuskowski, Alex. *Cool Eating: Healthy & Fun Ways to Eat Right.* Minneapolis, MN: ABDO Publishing, 2013.

WEBSITES

Fruit, Vegetables
www.freshforkids.com.au/fruit_pages/fruit.html
Want to know more about all kinds of fruit? Use this website!

Recipes
www.superhealthykids.com/healthy-kids-recipes.php
Check out this list of healthy, yummy recipes for all your meals!

Index